Original title:
Banana Bliss

Copyright © 2025 Creative Arts Management OÜ
All rights reserved.

Author: Nash Everly
ISBN HARDBACK: 978-1-80586-455-4
ISBN PAPERBACK: 978-1-80586-927-6

The Essence of Joy

In a peel of yellow, laughter hides,
A slip of joy where humor abides.
Jokes take flight on each fruity curve,
Joyful giggles, we all deserve.

Dancing monkeys in playful spree,
Swinging high, just like the trees.
With every bite, a chuckle grows,
Nature's treasure, in comical prose.

A Walk through the Grove

Strolling through trees of sunny cheer,
Giggles echo, oh so near.
Fruity friends with silly grins,
Whisper tales of playful spins.

On the ground, a peel takes flight,
A wobbly dance, what a sight!
Nature's laughter all around,
In the grove, pure joy is found.

Featherlight Fruits

Fluffy clouds and featherlight treats,
Bouncing joy in fruity beats.
With each taste, a chuckle flows,
Tickling senses, oh how it glows.

Wiggly giggles, playful bites,
Sunshine dances on summer nights.
In playful bowls, the humor swirls,
A feast of fun that twirls and twirls.

The Lure of the Tropics

In the tropics where laughter sings,
Witty fruit with silly flings.
Jokes are ripe, ready to peel,
Each fruity bite, a comedic deal.

Under palm trees, we share a grin,
Tropical breezes invite us in.
With zany shapes and quirky hues,
Joy takes root, in funny views.

Curved Joys

In a bowl they sit and grin,
Fruits of laughter, bright and thin.
Peeling back the sunny cheer,
They make all the bland things disappear.

Slip me on a comic ride,
Where morning giggles won't subside.
With each bite, a silly dance,
Taste of sunshine, pure romance.

Tropical Whispers

In the tropics, what a sight,
Coconuts and fruits delight.
Among them lies the cheerful kind,
With clever curves and smiles designed.

Swing around with comical flair,
Chasing giggles through the air.
A ripe reaction, what a tease,
You can't help but feel the ease.

A Peel of Happiness

Peel it back, what do we find?
A comical face so well-defined.
With every slice, a chuckle grows,
In this fruit, pure joy bestows.

Silly jokes and playful puns,
Whirling laughs like little runs.
Snack-time giggles, sweetness flows,
A fruity wave, it ebbs and goes.

Yellow Serenade

Golden hue, a cheerful song,
In juicy bites, we all belong.
Silly thoughts as laughter swells,
In the rhythm, joy compels.

Twist and turn, let's have some fun,
In every bite, a little pun.
With each munch, the giggles bloom,
Bringing smiles and dispelling gloom.

Light and Lush

In pajamas, I dance on the floor,
Peels slip by, oh, I adore.
Yellow smiles are my delight,
Swinging snacks in morning light.

Mischief lurking in each bite,
A fruit fight seems just so right.
Slipping quick with giggles bold,
Stories of the fruit unfold.

Luminous Harvests

Golden treasures in the sun,
Who knew this fruit could be such fun?
Falling laughter fills the air,
Chasing juice without a care.

Silly faces, sticky hands,
In this kingdom, laughter stands.
Every bite, a giggle burst,
In this feast, we quench our thirst.

Sweet Garden Whispers

In the garden's secret nook,
Lively critters, come take a look.
Chasing dreams on sunny hills,
Joy is found in fruity thrills.

Whispers soft of nature's cheer,
While munching snacks, we persevere.
Laughter echoes, fills the space,
With every nibble, find your place.

Gentle Ripeness

Soft and round, they smile so wide,
In their company, I won't hide.
Nibbles sweet, with giggles woven,
In this world, I'm freely chosen.

Under stars, we sing and sway,
Crafting fun in childlike play.
Each delight's a gentle treat,
Making moments feel complete.

A Toast to the Grove

In the grove where laughter blooms,
Fruitful pranks and silly tunes.
Slip and slide on peels so bright,
Chasing joy from day to night.

Yellow bunches sway and cheer,
Witty friends gathered near.
With each bite, a giggle's found,
Joyous echoes all around.

Lively Elixirs

Blend of flavors, mix it right,
Shake it up with all your might.
Sip the cheer, feel the thrill,
Fruity fun, let's drink our fill.

Silly straws and goofy hats,
Fluttering like playful cats.
Just one sip, and smiles appear,
Lively laughter fills the sphere.

Petals and Peels

Dancing petals in the breeze,
Peels create the silliest tease.
Slipping here, and tripping there,
Giggles bubble everywhere.

Nature's jest, the sun shines bright,
A playful game, pure delight.
With each slip, a funny tale,
In this garden, we prevail.

Harmony in Yellow

Cheerful hues fill up the air,
Waves of laughter everywhere.
Swaying shapes, a joyful dance,
In this mirth, we take a chance.

Golden fruits like rays of sun,
Every moment is pure fun.
In the feast of giggles sweet,
Life's a laugh with every treat.

Whimsical Harvest

In the orchard, yellow smiles grow,
Swinging high, what a fun show!
Monkeys chatter, swing with glee,
Happiness hangs from every tree.

Ripe and round, a silly sight,
Dancing fruits in morning light.
Juggling laughs, the air so sweet,
A fruity romp, no one can beat.

The Scent of Summer

Peels away worries, laughter spreads,
Beneath the shade, playful threads.
Giggling kids with sticky hands,
Joyful feasting on fruity strands.

Sunshine bursts, a fruity cheer,
Chasing shadows, we hold dear.
Every bite, a burst of fun,
Summer's magic, smiles begun.

Cheerful Crescendo

Up in the trees, they gleefully sway,
Whispering secrets, come out to play.
Slip and slide, a fruity fright,
Laughter echoes, pure delight.

Bouncing giggles, we all share,
Funky fruits dancing in the air.
Slide right in for a fruity feast,
Join the fun, be a happy beast!

Sunlit Succulence

Golden arcs in the bright blue sky,
Fuzzy faces, oh my, oh my!
Fickle fruits in a sunlit whirl,
Rolling round like a happy pearl.

Sticky fingers, whoops, we tripped,
Down the hill, the laughter slipped.
Savor sweetness in every bite,
Fun's the flavor, taste the light.

Yellow Serenade

In a fruit bowl they dance, all bright and bold,
With hats made of peel, tales to be told.
They slip and they slide, oh what a sight,
Chasing each other, day turns to night.

A jester's delight, they bounce off the wall,
With laughter and giggles, they're always on call.
In smoothies they sing, with a twist and a swirl,
Bringing a giggle to every young girl.

Symphony of Curves

With curves that invite, they march in a line,
Playing their tune, oh, so divine!
Each note a chuckle, in yellow attire,
They dance through the kitchen, setting hearts on fire.

A slip here and there, they freeze in their tracks,
Causing a ruckus, the laughter just cracks.
In salads they twirl, a fruity delight,
Joking with apples, oh what a night!

Nature's Sweet Surrender

In the sun they lounge, like kings on a throne,
Their peels golden bright, they're never alone.
With smiles that shine, they tickle the air,
A party of flavor, spreading joy everywhere.

Dropped from the tree, they tumble and roll,
Creating a fuss, like a comedy scroll.
They slip on a joke, with a giggle and cheer,
Inviting all creatures to join in the sphere.

Medley of Sunshine

In the garden they play, a lively brigade,
Tickling the taste buds, a fruity charade.
Each one a joker, so merry and bright,
Spreading pure joy with every bite.

They swing on the vines, with mischief in mind,
In the laughter of children, true bliss you will find.
Their antics are silly, a recipe grand,
Making life sweeter, just as they planned.

Curved Happiness

In the jungle, monkeys swing,
With giggles, loud they sing.
A fruit so bright, their favorite treat,
A snack that can't be beat.

Peels like slippers on the way,
One slip and down they'll sway!
They munch and cheer, it's quite the scene,
In their kingdom of green.

Laughter echoes through the trees,
A yellow feast that brings such glee.
With each bite, the joy expands,
As they dance in happy bands.

So if you see them leap and play,
Join the fun, don't delay!
For under the sun, with smiles so bold,
The tales of joy are made of gold.

Nature's Yellow Enchantment

In the sun, a golden glow,
Nature's jesters, steal the show.
With laughter sweet as morning dew,
They leap and twirl, a joyful crew.

A fruity slip, a comic treat,
Landing soft on tiny feet.
With giggles shared among the bunch,
Their wild games are quite the crunch.

Peels scatter like confetti bright,
As they dance with pure delight.
In every twist, a joke that's told,
In this grove, their hearts are bold.

Oh, come and taste the light-hearted cheer,
Where fun and friendship gather near!
In nature's arms, laughter soars,
A yellow charm that forever pours.

Sweet Surrender

In a picnic under trees,
Laughter floats upon the breeze.
A treat so sweet, it calls your name,
In this happy, fruity game.

A fellow trips and starts to tumble,
With a giggle, they all crumble.
The snacks fly high, a silly sight,
As their joy just feels so right.

Every munch, a cheerful cheer,
A fruit-filled day, oh so dear!
Their smiles stretch, as wide as can be,
In this world of pure glee.

So join the feast—don't be shy!
With every bite, laugh and sigh.
In this moment, all worries cease,
Surrender to the sweet, sweet peace.

Splendor of the Grove

Under the trees, the giggles rise,
Through the leaves, a merry surprise.
A yellow fruit, the crowd's delight,
In this grove, all feels so right.

They wear their peels like crowns of fun,
In a world where the sun has spun.
Each slip a tale, a laugh to share,
Friendship blooms in the sunny air.

Tumbling down, they land with grace,
Smiles plastered on every face.
The dance of life, so wild, so bold,
In this splendor, joy unfolds.

So gather round, come one, come all,
Join this feast, heed laughter's call!
In this grove, with hearts so free,
Eternal bliss is meant to be.

Blissful Bites

In a peel so bright and yellow,
Laughter leaps, a fruity fellow.
Chasing dreams, we munch with glee,
Silly faces, you and me.

Bouncing smiles with each soft bite,
Fruity giggles, pure delight.
Slipping on peels, we fall and play,
Who knew fruit could cause such sway?

A smoothie splash or pudding treat,
Dessert that dances on our feet.
Creamy bites of joy we share,
Forget your worries, shed your care.

So let's feast on nature's jest,
In every munch, we feel our best.
With every bite, more laughs ignite,
Oh, what a fruity, funny night!

Tropical Daydreams

Under sunbeams, we take a stroll,
Balmy breezes make us whole.
Fruity hats and silly shades,
Giggles echo in our parades.

Palm trees sway like dancers bold,
Stories of laughter, tales retold.
With every sip of juice we find,
Our sunny spirits intertwined.

Coconuts in toss and cheer,
All our jokes, we hold them dear.
While fruity vibes lighten the air,
Every moment we can't compare.

In tropical land, we wave and sway,
With laughter guiding all our play.
Sandy toes and sunshine's beams,
Awake in our fruity daydreams.

Colors of Cheer

A burst of color, a vibrant hue,
Fruit party fun, just me and you!
Giggles bloom like flowers bright,
In this kingdom of sheer delight.

Yellow splashes, tangy zest,
Every taste, we consider the best.
Twirling in shades of joy and art,
Together in flavors, we can't depart.

Sliced and diced, a carnival feast,
With fruity pals, we'll never cease.
Dancing dishes in bright array,
Cheerful laughter leads the way.

As we crunch, we paint the scene,
A joyous life, sweet and serene.
In every bite, we find our bliss,
With colorful joy that we can't miss!

Juicy Journeys

On a quest for sweetness, we embark,
With frolicsome footprints, we leave our mark.
Riding waves of zestful fun,
Chasing laughter, we just begun.

Slicing through rivers of juicy delight,
Splashing on shores, it feels just right.
With fruity maps, we chart our way,
Every giggle brightens the day.

Ripe adventures and silly spills,
Searching for joy that gives us thrills.
As we feast on nature's charm,
We hold each moment like a balm.

So pack your bags, let's dance and twirl,
In this juicy world, let laughter swirl.
Together we laugh, we sing, we play,
On a journey that brightens each day!

The Flavor of Paradise

In a land where yellow dreams grow,
The monkeys dance, putting on a show.
Peels slip and slide, oh what a sight,
Chasing their tails with pure delight.

With smoothies spun in a whirlpool's glee,
Milkshakes giggle, sweet as can be.
A fruit so funny, sweet and round,
Laughter echoes all around.

Jokes on the trees, they crack up loud,
As squirrels swing by, feeling so proud.
Happiness served on a leaf so wide,
Who knew that joy could come with a ride?

A feast for the senses, bright and bold,
With each creamy bite, stories unfold.
Tropical laughter fills the air,
In this paradise, you haven't a care.

Melodies of the Orchard

In the orchard, a tune takes flight,
As critters croon throughout the night.
Swinging vines in a jazzy dance,
Fruits jive along, give it a chance.

A plucky tune that makes you grin,
With melodies from where they've been.
Each juicy note a burst of cheer,
Come join the fun, it's time, my dear.

The swing of fruit makes the squirrels sway,
While bees bop in, making their way.
Nature's concert, what a fine treat,
Grab a seat, feel the fruity beat.

Quirky rhythms from a fruity band,
Green leaves echo with laughter so grand.
Serenade of sunshine, sweet and bright,
In this orchard, all feels just right.

Under the Fruitful Canopy

Beneath the leaves, a world so bright,
Where laughter lives, and dreams take flight.
A canopy whispering to the breeze,
Tickles the nose with such sweet Glee.

The rustling fruit sings silly songs,
As critters gather, where everyone belongs.
A picnic spread with smiles galore,
You never knew fruit could cause such uproar.

A splat here, a slip there, giggles unfold,
Sunshine spills like laughter untold.
A whimsical realm where joy shimmies by,
In this fruity playground, happiness is nigh.

Here's to the fun, so carefree and bright,
With every bite, we dance in delight.
Under the branches, we revel and play,
Join this jolly fun, come hang out today!

Savoring Sunshine

Oh, what a feast of golden delight,
With sunshine wrapped, oh, what a sight!
Smiles blossom like flowers in spring,
Each slice a tune that makes hearts sing.

Slipping on peels makes giggles ignite,
As laughter sprinkles the warm daylight.
Creamy concoctions spinning around,
In sunny laughter, joy can be found.

The fruit parade is all the rage,
With monkeys leading a fruity stage.
Life's little quirks in every bite,
In this fruity frenzy, everything's right.

Savor the moments, make them last,
As the sun dips low, and shadows are cast.
In this world where silliness reigns,
Happiness flows like sweet summer rains.

Fruity Euphoria

In a land of yellow cheer,
The peels have tales to share.
Every bite a giggle spree,
With smoothies flying everywhere.

Silly slips on polished floors,
Comedians of the fruit old score.
They dance around with joyful cries,
In this fruity world, laughter flies.

A snack that makes the tummy cheer,
One bite and you'll jump dear,
The creaminess with a twist of glee,
Makes every bland moment carefree.

So let's toast with all our might,
To the fruit that brings pure delight.
In every corner, joy's unfurled,
This zany fruit takes over the world.

Nature's Curved Wonder

Oh, nature's curvy little gift,
With a yellow smile, it gives a lift.
In the morning sun, it swings and sways,
A fruity prankster that loves to play.

At the picnic, it's the star,
With laughter ringing near and far.
Peel away worries, grab a bite,
This cheeky treat makes life feel right.

It rolls along, so full of bliss,
Unexpected joy with every kiss.
Make a cake, or just munch it whole,
This fruity friend will lift your soul.

So here's to the fun in every taste,
In this sweet world, there's no time to waste.
Nature's laughter in every cream,
A happy fruit, living the dream.

Lush Harvests

In lush fields beneath the sun,
Harvest time means fruity fun.
With baskets filled and smiles so wide,
Let's take a stroll, let joy reside.

Each curve a moment, ripe and bright,
Every munch brings pure delight.
Sliced in bowls or shaking shakes,
This joyful fruit, it never fakes.

With every wink and every charm,
A fruity hug that warms the calm.
So grab a friend and let's unite,
For harvest time is pure sunshine.

Let's make a feast, a wacky spread,
With laughter bubbling like fresh bread.
In the heart of summer's game,
This playful treat is never lame.

Sun-Kissed Dreams

Beneath a sky so blue and bright,
Sun-kissed dreams take their flight.
With little laughs and silly schemes,
In a fruity world where nothing seems.

Chasing shadows, we set the pace,
Each yellow treasure leaves a trace.
A bite that giggles, a peel that grins,
In this juicy land, nobody wins.

Let's swing from trees, embrace the cheer,
With every snack, we spread good cheer.
This fruit is magic, pure and free,
A sweet reminder of glee for me.

Roll on laughter, roll on fun,
With every yellow snack, we run.
In sun-kissed lands where joy plants dreams,
Who knew such bliss could burst at seams?

Simple Pleasures

Peeling back that yellow skin,
A fruit that's sure to make us grin.
With every bite, a funny twist,
A happiness that can't be missed.

Slip on down, oh what a sight,
A joyous dance, pure delight.
Sticky fingers, laughter's cheer,
Who knew fruit could bring such gear?

Bananarama, do a jig,
Watch them roll, so fun and big.
In smoothie or a cake so bright,
These yellow treats bring pure delight.

From monkey's dreams to morning snacks,
They make us smile, no need for hacks.
So here's to joy in every bite,
A silly fruit, a true delight.

Childhood Reverie

Once in a tree, I made my throne,
With yellow treasures all my own.
Swinging high, I'd shout with glee,
These cheerful snacks belong to me!

The laughter echoed, wild and free,
A slip so grand, oh can't you see?
Skid marks on pavement, a playful chase,
The perfect landing, oh what a place!

I'd munch and crunch in sunny light,
With friends around, what pure delight.
Backyard picnics, squeals so bright,
In every bite, a taste of flight.

Childhood days like fleeting dreams,
In every laugh, laughter teems.
So raise a toast to yellow cheer,
Those fruity days we hold so dear.

The Orchard's Song

Under the trees, such shades of fun,
The laughter flows, just like the sun.
With plump delights hanging in glee,
Nature's treasures, come climb with me!

Each little bite brings joy divine,
A twist of humor in every line.
Juicy laughter in every peel,
A fruit-tastic meal, oh what a deal!

Out in the meadow, let's run and play,
Silly games throughout the day.
With bouncy fruits that bring a grin,
Let's gather round and dig right in!

The orchard hums a tune so bright,
Dancing shadows in warm daylight.
So sing along, don't be shy,
With every giggle, let's reach the sky!

Sunlit Savorings

Golden rays upon my face,
A little fruit brings a funny grace.
With smoothies whirling, oh so sweet,
A joyful harvest, quite the treat.

On picnic blankets, we all sit,
Bantering back, we laugh a bit.
With silly faces at every turn,
In fruity splendor, there's much to learn!

The sun dips low, the laughter swells,
With every bite, the fervor dwells.
We share our tales, we share our fun,
Under bright skies, we come undone.

So top it off with laughter grand,
Each fruity hug, a playful hand.
With sunlit savorings, we toast,
To fruity smiles we love the most!

Golden Delight

In the morning sun, so bright and bold,
A yellow treasure, ripe and gold.
With a peel so slick, I take a bite,
A silly grin, pure delight.

Monkeys swing, they laugh and play,
Chasing dreams in a fruity way.
With every munch, I can't help but smile,
This magic fruit, oh, it's worth my while.

Slipping on peels, a comical sight,
Each tumble brings giggles, oh what a night!
The tropics sing with this cheerful tune,
As I dance around like a jovial loon.

So here's to joy, in every bite,
A fruity romance that feels so right.
With laughter and fun, we share the feast,
Celebrating life, a joyous beast!

Whispers of the Tropics

In the cool shade of palm tree trees,
Whispers of laughter carried by the breeze.
A yellow orb, hanging with glee,
Calls for a snack, just wait and see!

With every munch, flavors collide,
Silly moments, we cannot hide.
From smoothies to splits, it's never a chore,
This joyful fruit, we always adore!

Under the sun, we frolic and roll,
Bouncing about, losing control.
Each slippery step, oh what a thrill,
Squeals of laughter, we can't get our fill!

So lift your glass, let's toast and cheer,
To fruity adventures that bring us near.
In this tropical land, we find our fun,
With our yellow buddies, we're never done!

Sunny Slips

A slip on a peel, what a sight to see,
As I tumble and giggle, oh woe is me!
The sun above casts a golden glow,
Chasing my worries, back to where they grow.

There's mischief afoot, in every bite,
From smoothies to shakes, it's pure delight.
As flavors dance, tickling my tongue,
This bright fruit's praises will always be sung.

At picnics we gather, a feasting crew,
Sharing laughter, both fresh and anew.
With fruity jokes, that can't be missed,
We raise our hands to the yellow bliss!

So come join the fun, grab a bunch in hand,
In this silly circus, take a stand.
With joy in our hearts, and slips guaranteed,
We'll dance like monkeys, oh yes indeed!

The Fruitful Reverie

In a dreamlike land where yellow beams shine,
Fruits frolic freely, oh so divine.
With giggles and whispers that fill the air,
A whimsical world of fruity flair.

Each slice brings laughter, a sweet surprise,
Dancing in rhythm, we cheer and rise.
From popsicles bright to sundaes fair,
The joy of this fruit, beyond compare!

As monkeys exchange their cheeky grins,
We gobble the joy, where the fun begins.
With every chuckle, and every cheer,
Life feels lighter, as sunshine draws near.

So lift your voices and break into song,
In this sunny paradise, you'll never go wrong.
A celebration of flavors, hilarious indeed,
In our fruitful reverie, we all take heed!

Luminescent Harvest

In the orchard where smiles grow,
Yellow fruits dance in the glow.
Beneath the leaves, laughter spills,
Swinging in joy, with silly thrills.

Ripe and ready, they start to sway,
Tickling hearts in a playful way.
Each one grins, a cheeky tease,
Chasing away any hint of unease.

On a breeze, the stories float,
Nonsense murmurs, a merry note.
Peeled and shared with merry cheer,
Bananas twinkle, spreading good cheer.

So let us gather, sing out loud,
Join the fun, embrace the crowd.
For in this harvest of pure delight,
Every bite is a giggling sight.

Chasing Yellow Shadows

In the sunlight, shadows caper,
Chasing joy with every paper.
Curved and bright, they leap around,
Creating giggles, a merry sound.

With each twist, they play a game,
Hiding, seeking, never the same.
Beneath the trees, the fun ignites,
Golden smiles and playful flights.

Eyes so gleeful, spirits high,
Rolling laughter, oh my, oh my!
A silly dance, a twist, a turn,
In this yellow shade, we laugh and yearn.

So grab a friend and take a chance,
Join the fruit in a happy dance.
In the chase of those sunny rays,
Every moment is a laugh-filled maze.

Sunshine on the Palate

A slice of sun on a bright white plate,
Laughter bubbles, oh isn't it great?
With every bite, joy fills the air,
Sweetness tickles, a light affair.

Creamy textures, the spoon takes flight,
Morsels of laughter, pure delight.
Cheery flavors, swirling fun,
In the kitchen, we're never done.

Chop and mix, create the cheer,
Every taste a chuckle, loud and clear.
Spoonfuls of happiness, piled high,
Joyful rhythms as we all abide.

So gather round, the table's set,
Moments of sweetness, we won't forget.
For in this feast, we surely find,
Sunshine lingers, delightfully blind.

Sweet Laughter in Every Bite

In every nibble, giggles burst,
Flavorful fun, oh what a thirst!
A twist of cheer, a scoop of joy,
Laughter dances, never coy.

With a wink and a playful nib,
Every munch, a funny fib.
Silly faces, twinkling eyes,
Around the table, hilarity flies.

Spread the joy on a toasted slice,
Each little morsel is so nice.
A splendid treat, this playful bite,
Bringing smiles, a pure delight.

So take a spoon, don't be shy,
Indulge in laughter, come on, let's try.
For in this feast, we all unite,
Sweet giggles linger, feeling just right.

Adrift in Fruitfulness

A bunch of yellow smiles, I see,
Swinging on trees, wild and free.
With peels like slippers, soft and bright,
They dance in the sun, a pure delight.

Chasing after monkeys, oh what fun!
They giggle and squeal, until they're done.
In smoothies swirled, or cakes that rise,
These fruits bring laughter, no surprise!

Floating on rivers of creamy dreams,
With sticky fingers and chocolate streams.
I tuck one in my pocket, just in case,
For a sunny snack or a monkey chase!

So let us feast, on this lively treat,
In every bite, joy feels complete.
With every munch, a cheeky grin,
In a fruity world, let the fun begin!

Radiant Gatherings

A party of flavors, bright and bold,
In tropical shades, stories unfold.
With fruity hats and a splash of cheer,
These gatherings spark smiles far and near.

Sipping on smoothies, the laughter flows,
While juggling fruit, we strike silly poses.
A peel rolls away, laughter ensues,
Oh, who can resist these playful hues?

Join in the fun, take a gooey bite,
Sweetness exploding, pure delight.
As we dance beneath the sun so bright,
Our flavors twirl, in joyous flight!

So come on over, gather around,
In this fruity kingdom, happiness is found.
With every giggle, every hearty cheer,
We'll celebrate flavors, year after year!

Sweet Rhapsody

In a land of twirling, tasty dreams,
Where laughter mingles with fruity themes.
Elixir of joy in every bite,
Life becomes a rhapsody, pure delight.

With cream and honey, we compose a song,
Each slice a note, where we belong.
Dancing through bowls, a fruity parade,
With prancing peels, we're never afraid!

The giggles bubble like fizzy drinks,
As taste buds cheer, and nobody thinks.
What a zesty world, where flavors play,
In a symphony sweet, we laugh all day!

So come let's gather, sing loud and clear,
In our fruity concert, there's nothing to fear.
With sticky tongues and joyful hearts,
This sweet rhapsody, where fun never departs!

The Color of Happiness

In shades of sunshine, smiles arise,
With giggles painting joy in the skies.
Golden treasures in every snack,
A playful treat, never looking back.

Rolling on tables, we share our feast,
A colorful party, joy unleashed.
With pops of flavor and endless glee,
The fruit parade dances wild and free!

Stickers and sprinkles adorn every plate,
As sweet surprises make us celebrate.
Laughter echoes, a colorful song,
In this tasty world, we all belong!

So grab a slice, let the fun ignite,
In this garden of happiness, pure delight.
With every nibble, our spirits will soar,
Join the merry feast, we'll always want more!

Whispers of the Tropics

In the land where fruit does play,
Yellow smiles greet the day.
Monkeys giggle in the trees,
Swinging softly in the breeze.

Juicy laughter fills the air,
With each bite, a fruity dare.
Slip and slide on peels of cheer,
Come and join us, have no fear!

A smoothie party, oh what fun!
Dancing shadows in the sun.
Silly hats atop our heads,
Tropical dreams on cozy beds.

So gather 'round, let's raise a toast,
To the fruit we love the most.
In this joyful, sunny scene,
Life's a party, bright and green!

A Tropical Escape

Palm trees sway, the sun's our guide,
With fruity treats, we take a ride.
Giggles echo through the sand,
Life's a feast, just as we planned!

Coconuts and fruity pies,
Glassy waves beneath the skies.
Run and slip, it's quite a sight,
Tropical laughs last through the night.

Mango hats and lemon shorts,
Join our carnival of sorts.
A parade of flavors, pure delight,
Come on, friends, let's shine so bright!

As the sun begins to set,
We'll dance and laugh, no need to fret.
With every bite, the fun expands,
Let's escape to these warm sands!

Lighthearted Indulgence

Whipped cream towers in delight,
Splat! A pie takes off in flight!
Topping treats on every plate,
Who can resist? It feels like fate!

Slippery peels, be cautious, friend,
Laughter's waiting 'round the bend.
Sundaes stacked, oh what a scene,
Join the fun, live the dream!

Pineapple stacks, they reach so high,
Loop-de-loops as flavors fly.
Let's create a tasty mess,
In this joyful, fruity dress!

So grab a friend, and let's be bold,
With giggles and treats, we'll break the mold.
In this sweet world, we find our bliss,
Come indulge in our whimsical kiss!

Carefree Gatherings

A picnic spread, oh what a treat,
Banded chairs and fruity feet.
Cake slices fly, a sweet delight,
Cracks me up 'til I take flight!

Tropical tunes play on repeat,
Here we giggle, here we greet.
Splat! A splash, confusion reigns,
Let's embrace all happy gains!

With each nibble, laughter curls,
Silly games and jumping swirls.
Colorful hats and bright balloons,
Join the fun, forget your tunes!

At sunset's glow, we toast with cheer,
For fruity friends and hearty beer.
In our carefree, crazy land,
Together we will always stand!

Laughter Wrapped in Yellow

In the kitchen, peels do dance,
A fruity twist, a wobbly prance.
They slip and slide, oh what a sight,
A jester's treat in morning light.

Muffins rise with glee so bright,
A yellow smile, oh what a bite!
Frolic with a spoon, make a mess,
Each scoop a giggle, pure happiness.

Twirling spoons in a fruity whirl,
Is there any joy that can unfurl?
They laugh with every silly taste,
A fruity feast, none is waste.

Join the fun, don't be shy,
With every bite, reach for the sky.
Here's to laughter, sweet and cheery,
In every snack, be bright and merry.

A Slice of Joy

Slice it thick or slice it thin,
Each piece brings a cheeky grin.
Packed with giggles, sweet delight,
Every mouthful feels just right.

Creamy spreads and crunchy bites,
With every taste, the joy ignites.
On toasts or bowls, let's make a cheer,
Laughing loudly, the end is near!

Let's make a smoothie, whip it fast,
Blend the laughter, have a blast!
The funny faces that we wear,
Sip and snort without a care.

More than meals, it's moments shared,
The joy of sharing, none compared.
So raise your glass, make it bright,
With slices of joy that feel just right.

Vibrant Nectar

Splash of yellow in the blender,
Swirl it round, let's be a contender!
Sippin' sundaes, oh what fun,
Chasing flavors, we won't run.

With smoothies thick and toppings tall,
Who said dessert can't enthrall?
A sprinkle here, a drizzle there,
In this nectar, laughter's rare.

Meringue and whip, the dance begins,
Chefs and jokers, battling wins!
Facial expressions, all askew,
Oh, what fun when it's mixed askew!

Cheers to nectar we all adore,
More fun with every pour!
Raise your cups to joy anew,
In vibrant flavors, we pursue.

Summertime Splendor

Under the sun, we gather 'round,
With fruity treats and laughter sound.
Picnic dreams with giggles wide,
A summer vibe we cannot hide.

Wobbly drinks in goofy cups,
Our silly cheers, can't get enough!
With every sip, our spirits soar,
In this arena, we laugh galore.

Catch a splash, the fruits collide,
Every taste a silly ride!
From playful pies to creamy shakes,
Our laughter spreads, oh how it breaks!

So let's bask in sunny days,
In silly snacks and playful ways.
With smiles and bites that never end,
In summertime splendor, joy will blend.

Garden of Fruitful Dreams

In the garden where fruits all play,
A yellow delight shouts, 'Hooray!'
With laughter and giggles it swings,
Sharing joy that each moment brings.

The critters all join in the fun,
Dancing 'round like they've just begun.
The shadows twist for a silly show,
A feast of humor where laughter flows.

Fruit flies giggle, they zip and zoom,
As they crash on a big fruit boom.
A splash of juice, what a sight!
Let's squeeze it in, with all our might!

So join the crew, do not delay,
In this garden, we'll laugh and play.
With jokes and puns that never cease,
In fruity lands, we find our peace.

Tropical Euphoria

Under palm trees, warm and bright,
Yellow critters steal the night.
Wiggling tails and giggles abound,
In the tropics, joy is found.

Fruits twirl 'round in a happy dance,
With every leap, they take a chance.
A zesty breeze brings silly cheer,
As mischief blooms, the end is near!

With coconut hats, they strut with pride,
Joking and jiving, side by side.
Splashes of juice, they chuck and toss,
In this laughter, we can't be lost.

The sun dips low, it's time to play,
Join the crew, don't shy away.
In tropical lands where the fun won't cease,
Together we find our fruity peace.

The Joyful Peel

Peeling back with a funny twist,
A yellow friend can't be missed!
Slipping, sliding, right off the vine,
It stumbles forward, oh so divine!

Laughter erupts as it trips and rolls,
With giggles that tickle our very souls.
A fruity romp through the high grass,
Who'd have thought, such joy would amass?

In every leaf, a chuckle's found,
As we dance on this silly ground.
Banished frowns, all joy unveiled,
With every bite, our worries curtailed.

So peel away the serious guise,
With each funny slip, we'll rise.
A world where laughter is the deal,
In every bite, the joy's revealed!

Delectable Dancer

In the kitchen, things get wild,
A twisty treat that's brightly styled.
Sass and flavor with every beat,
A delectable dancer that can't be beat!

It twirls on counters, what a sight,
With laughter echoing through the night.
Giggling mayhem, it leaps and bounds,
With every jig, pure joy abounds.

Watch it whirl in a fruity spree,
Bouncing 'round like it's full of glee.
A peel here, a chuckle there,
With every dance, we cease to care.

So join the dance, don't miss a chance,
Let's all partake in this silly prance.
In this kitchen, we shimmer and shine,
With delectable moves that taste divine!

A Dance of Curves

In the kitchen, fruits collide,
A yellow fruit with so much pride.
It wiggles, jiggles on the floor,
Saying, 'Come on, let's dance some more!'

With a peel that's bright and bold,
Its laughter is worth more than gold.
It rolls and tumbles all around,
Creating giggles, such sweet sound.

Not just a snack, it's full of cheer,
It makes you smile, brings you near.
Oh, the joy it brings today,
In a wacky, fruity play!

Let's celebrate this sunny treat,
Its antics make our lives complete.
Bring on the fun, let's laugh and sing,
This fruit, my friend, is a wondrous thing!

Fruity Fantasia

Under the sun, so bright, so warm,
Lives a fruit that charms with its form.
It twirls in the breeze, all yellow and neat,
A comical wonder, a funny little treat.

In the basket, it creates a scene,
A fruity party, oh so keen!
It slides and glides; it can't sit still,
Rendering everyone with a thrill.

When it splits, we giggle loud,
This cheerful character draws a crowd.
From smoothies to pies, it rules the day,
In a most delightful, fruity display!

So take a bite, and feel the fun,
This yellow delight is second to none.
With every chomp, you'll join the cheer,
A fruity fantasia, let's all draw near!

The Essence of Delight

Peeling back layers, what do we find?
A treasure that tickles, oh so kind.
It's yellow, it's silly, a perfect sight,
Bringing giggles from morning till night.

With a squish and a squeeze, it sings a tune,
This zany fruit makes us swoon.
In a smoothie or split, joy takes flight,
A comical romp, pure delight!

Dancing on plates, it winks all around,
As we all gather, laughter is found.
This fragrant wonder, a true delight,
In every party, it shines so bright!

So let's spread cheer with this cheerful fruit,
In every bite, there's joy to boot.
Celebrate the essence, take a big slice,
This quirky delight is oh-so-nice!

Tropical Bounty

In the tropical sun, it gleams with flair,
A chattering fruit, light as air.
It knows how to have a jolly good time,
Bringing laughter, pure delight with each rhyme.

It may look serious, in a funny way,
But when you taste it, it's here to play!
A splash of sweetness, a whimsical twist,
This cheerful treasure is hard to resist.

With a curve that's catchy and so absurd,
It tickles your fancy, this clever bird.
In salads or shakes, it'll charm your face,
This fruity bounty is a happy place!

So gather your friends, let the fun unfold,
With this quirky delight, be brave and bold.
In the tropical heat, let the laughter flow,
A bounty of joy, come join the show!

Dancing with Delight

In the kitchen, pots and pans,
Fruits are jiving, take a chance.
Spinning round in fruity cheer,
Laughs abound, there's joy so near.

Slipping on a peel or two,
Oops! There goes my dance debut.
Funky moves and giggles free,
Groovin' like it's meant to be.

Salsa with the yellow curve,
Twists and twirls, we've got the nerve.
Pineapples join, they sway with glee,
A fruity jam, just you and me.

When the music starts to play,
Who needs a cake? We'll dance away.
Laughter bursts, we twirl and glide,
In this party, fruit's our pride.

Orchard's Embrace

In the orchard where joy grows,
Fruit hangs low, a sunny pose.
Bouncing off the branches wide,
Nature's giggles, take a ride.

A parrot on a branch so high,
Tells a joke and makes us sigh.
Lemons laugh, and so do we,
Who knew fruit could bring such glee?

With a basket full of dreams,
We're picking up the silliest schemes.
Berries burst with laughter bright,
In this orchard, all feels right.

Crickets sing their nightly tune,
Underneath the glowing moon.
In this place, we dance and sway,
Orchard's charm, come out to play!

Bright Bounty

A sunlit stage, the fruits align,
Grapes are rolling like a fine wine.
Limes are zesty, lemons grin,
In this bounty, we all win.

A mango slips, not so stealth,
We giggle at its fruity self.
Plums collide in joyful cheer,
A fruity party, loud and clear.

With each crunch, a burst of fun,
Crisp and juicy, we have won.
Orange slices, a merry crew,
Squeezing laughter, me and you.

The picnic spreads a funny sight,
Watermelon, oh what a delight!
In every bite, there's joy, we find,
A bright bounty, fruit intertwined.

The Cheerful Tapestry

Woven tales of fruit so bright,
Strawberries dance in pure delight.
Happiness stitched on every slice,
Their cheerful colors, oh so nice.

Fabric soft with fruity scents,
Pineapples giggle, no pretense.
Apples twirl in vibrant threads,
Dancing through our sleepy heads.

Banquet spread, a festive view,
Every plate a canvas, too.
Juicy laughter, fabrics blend,
Together here, the fun won't end.

With each bite, a story told,
Of fruity joys, both brave and bold.
In this cheerful tapestry,
Life's a party, just let it be!

Laughter in the Orchard

In the shade of a tree, there's a sound,
A giggle erupts from the ground.
Fruit on the vine, swinging high,
Each time it drops, it makes me sigh.

The squirrels join in, they dance and play,
Chasing around, they brighten the day.
With peels on the grass, the jokes have begun,
Twirling and laughing, oh what fun!

A slip, a fall, oh look at that!
Harvest-time comedy, how funny is that?
Giggles and grins, all around,
In this orchard, joy can be found.

So gather the friends, let laughter grow,
In fruity chaos, the fun will flow.
Slice up a grin, enjoy the breeze,
In the heart of the orchard, we do as we please.

Citrus Kiss of Summer

Golden rays burst through the trees,
With laughter that dances upon the breeze.
A splash of juice, what a funny sight,
Sticky fingers, oh what a delight!

Lemon and lime, they wink with glee,
Spritzing a splash, 'Come play with me!'
Silly hats made from the tangy rinds,
Wobbling on heads, oh what finds!

Jumping through puddles of juice so sweet,
Dancing in chaos, oh, what a treat!
Citrus kisses in the summer sun,
Laughter erupts, the day's just begun!

So raise a toast with fruity cheer,
Embrace the humor year after year.
In this summer glow, we play and sing,
With a citrus twist—the joy it brings!

Curves of Joy

Round and plump, they sway on trees,
Curvy treasures whisper in the breeze.
A playful dance, around they go,
With silly hats, it's quite the show!

Friends gather close to take a peek,
At the whimsical shapes that make us squeak.
One takes a tumble, giggles spread wide,
In this fruity world, laughter's our guide.

Bouncing about in a joyful spree,
Rolling and tumbling, oh how carefree!
Curved like smiles, they light up the day,
With each little squish, we giggle and play.

So treasure the laughter, embrace the fun,
In the garden of joy, we're never done.
With curves of delight, let's sing again,
In this whimsical dance, we'll always remain!

Radiant Harvest

Under the sun, it's a radiant day,
With fruits that shimmer and sway.
A basket full of giggles to share,
Joyful chaos is everywhere!

Picking with friends, what a bright scene,
Spilling the goods, oh what a meme!
Fruits tumble down, creating a mess,
Yet every slip brings more happiness.

From tree to table, it's a fruity race,
With laughter echoing in this happy place.
Silly faces and sticky fingers,
Smiles grow wide as the joy lingers.

So gather your friends for this harvest cheer,
With every chuckle, we bring them near.
In the glow of the sun, let the fun ignite,
For in this moment, everything feels right!

Teardrops of Sunshine

A yellow fruit with a funny peel,
It slips away, oh such a steal!
I grin as I take a feisty bite,
My morning starts with pure delight.

It makes a smoothie, what a scene,
With dancing colors, like a dream.
The laughter echoes, can't contain,
As I slip and slide in morning rain.

A monkey's snack, they can't resist,
In every lunchbox, a fruity twist.
I throw it high, just for some fun,
But it lands square on my dad's bun!

So here's to joy, in every bunch,
Life's better with a yellow munch.
With giggles and smiles, let's all unite,
For laughter served with every bite!

Radiance in Every Bite

A golden crescent in my hand,
It brings sunshine, oh so grand.
In cereal or pie, it's quite the treat,
My goofy grin can't be beat!

The garden's treasure, laughter blooms,
As I juggle with fruity plumes.
It makes me dance a silly jig,
While slipping on this fruit so big!

Each squishy bite brings joy anew,
Splatters of flavor, bright yellow hue.
In smoothies or bread, we can't ignore,
A little giggle—Oh, what's in store?

So let's cheer for this funny fruit,
With its sunny face oh what a hoot!
As long as it's ripe, I'll take a chomp,
And laugh every time I take a stomp!

Mellow Moods

A gentle curve with a sassy grin,
This fruity treasure pulls me in.
It whispers softly to my heart,
With every munch, we play our part.

Bananas swing on kitchen hooks,
They tease the chef with comic looks.
In pancakes high, it plays a role,
Making mornings bright and whole.

Peel it back, what a surprise,
A sunny fruit that never lies.
In cakes or shakes, it finds a way,
To brighten up the dullest day!

With every bite, there's laughter found,
A quirky fruit, so round and sound.
With gentleness, this snack is sweet,
Joy dances on my cheerful feet!

The Flavorful Symphony

A fruity fling, a peppy cheer,
The joy of snacks that draws us near.
In puddings, pops, or straight alone,
A tasty serenade that's fully grown.

With every slice, the comedy swells,
As I slip on peels like tiny spells.
Juggling fruits, I'm quite the sight,
Embracing giggles with each bite.

A sprinkle here, a dash of flair,
This gold is dancing everywhere.
In smoothies mixed, a laughter spree,
This fruity tune is pure decree!

So raise a slice, let's celebrate,
For fruity fun we cultivate.
Let voices rise in laughter's game,
For every bite, we share the fame!

A Taste of Paradise

In the tree the yellow gems hang,
Swinging low, they dance and clang.
A monkey's feast, a cheeky grin,
With every bite, the laughter begins.

Peel it down, a slippery race,
Whoops! I slipped on my own face!
With squeaks and giggles, we all play,
A fruity joy that saves the day.

Creamy treats on plates we line,
With silly faces, all divine.
Chasing dreams of pudding sweet,
A circus of flavors, can't be beat!

So here we stand, in sunny cheer,
With fruity smiles, and lots of beer!
We toast to fun, oh what a trip,
This zany fruit, we just can't quit!

Sun-Kissed Delight

In the sun, we stake our claim,
Frosty drinks, a zesty game.
We gather round to share the joy,
Oh, how we giggle, girls and boys!

A smoothie splash, a funny roar,
As fruits collide, we all implore.
Whoops! More splatters on my shirt!
But what's the fuss? It's fruit dessert!

We craft all things, from fries to pies,
But laughter shines through all our tries.
With every bite, a wacky scheme,
Our funny feast, oh what a dream!

Friends and flavors in the sun,
In this crazy game, we're all one.
With fruit hats on, we're out of sight,
Let's dance it out, till the moon is bright!

Golden Delights

Oh, golden curves in a sunny pack,
Rolling on wheels, oh what a hack!
We juggle them high, drop with a thunk,
These fruity wonders, they never stunk!

In the kitchen, mayhem rules,
With giggles mixed like silly fools.
A scoop of joy, we laugh and yell,
This golden treasure casts a spell!

We wear the peels like crowns of gold,
Playing tricks never gets old.
With every munch, the chuckles flow,
What a delight, this showbiz show!

So come along, it's quite a sight,
A party of fruit, all day and night.
With silly games, our spirits soar,
In this fruity life, we ask for more!

The Sweetness of Sunlight

Warmed by rays, we weave our tale,
With squishy bites that never pale.
Each little chunk, a burst of cheer,
Silly faces, we hold dear!

In a fruit bowl, all things collide,
Crazy colors, side by side.
With every munch, a funny face,
Fruity giggles fill the space!

We squeeze and mash, what a delight,
Creating treats that feel just right.
In our laughter, we find the fun,
Chasing rays, we never run!

So grab a slice, let's celebrate,
With every bite, our joy's innate.
Sunny sweetness, oh what a blast,
In this fruity fun, we hold fast!

Sweet Whirlwind

In the kitchen, a slip and slide,
Yellow fruit takes us for a ride.
Jokes on the peels, laughter will spill,
As we munch and giggle, it's quite the thrill.

A fruit with curves that dance in sight,
Chasing after dreams, oh, what a fright!
Smoothies whirl like a merry-go-round,
With creamy laughter, bliss can be found.

Splashing in pancakes, a comedy twist,
Maple syrup hopes it won't be missed.
With every bite, there's a chuckle shared,
Joyous moments, nothing compared!

So sway with the rhythm, take note of this,
For fruity fun, you cannot dismiss.
Wrapped in laughter, the world's a spin,
Embrace the sweet joy hiding within.

Festive Foliage

In the garden, a party bright,
Leaves are dancing, what a sight!
Bunches hang like laughter on vines,
While mischief hops from frond to pines.

Curtains of green with yellow splotches,
Holding secrets like little botches.
With every munch, the chuckles rise,
As fruity surprises dance in our eyes.

Oh, tickle my taste buds, what a tease,
As sunshine drips from leafy trees.
Juicy smiles in every bite,
Spreading fun, morning to night!

So here's to the party, we all partake,
With fruity fun, for laughter's sake.
Jump and dance in the foliage bright,
Nature's humor brings pure delight!

Sunshine on a Plate

A splash of yellow, round and sweet,
Climbing higher than a happy feat.
On our plates like a sunbeam bright,
Tickling senses in pure delight.

Baked in muffins, or whipped in cream,
Creating a life, all in a dream.
As cocoa kisses with laughter's grace,
Moments of joy fully embrace.

With friends around, we laugh and share,
The sticky fingers, we don't care.
Each slice brings smiles, a funny sight,
Carved with love, our hearts take flight.

So lift your fork for this tasty treat,
A slice of sunshine can't be beat.
Chasing away the clouds so gray,
With giggles and munchies, hip hip hooray!

Nature's Golden Gift

A treasure hidden in leaves of green,
A playful fruit that's rarely seen.
Hopping onto plates with a giggle loud,
Making everyone laugh, drawing a crowd.

Ripening under the sun's warm rays,
It crafts smiles in oh-so-many ways.
From smoothies to splits, it takes a bow,
Stealing the show, oh wow wow wow!

With each peeled layer, joy unfurls,
Golden delights to share with the world.
A tickle of flavor, fruity and bright,
Bouncing on tongues, oh what a sight!

So let's scoop it up, one by one,
Join the feast, oh what fun!
With laughter shared and spirits high,
Nature's gift will never lie.

The Art of Sweetness

In a peel so bright, a smile grows wide,
Fling it in the air, let joy be the ride.
Slip on a slice, what a sight to see,
Giggles erupt, oh, life's wild spree.

Cakes and treats, they all can't compare,
To the fruit of laughter, light as the air.
A splash on the plate, joy never tires,
With each little bite, it fuels our desires.

Vibrancy Unleashed

Yellow like sunshine, so totally bright,
Juggling this snack brings pure delight.
Wobbly on legs, I take a sweet stand,
Who knew such magic could fit in my hand?

With every soft bite, a chuckle takes flight,
It's messy and fun, everything feels right.
A fruit that goes crazy, it dances with glee,
In the circus of flavors, come join with me!

Everyday Euphoria

Mornings burst forth with a golden ray,
Grab it and laugh, it's a goofy buffet.
Mash it on toast, or eat it whole,
This quirky little treat brings joy to the soul.

In smoothies it spins like a dizzying dream,
A slice on pizza? An absurd new theme!
The humor it brings, like a peek-a-boo game,
Fun with this fruit, nothing feels the same.

The Golden Cascade

Raining down sweetness from the grove of glee,
Peels that entice, come share them with me!
A slip and a flop, chaos is near,
With every misstep, we burst out in cheer.

Pack on the laughter, we all take a dive,
In puddles of joy, oh, how we thrive!
Golden and goofy, our spirits take flight,
In the world of the silly, everything feels right.

www.ingramcontent.com/pod-product-compliance
Lightning Source LLC
Chambersburg PA
CBHW070004300426
43661CB00141B/217